Slices of Life

Anvi K

BookLeaf Publishing

India | USA | UK

Presentation by *BookLeaf Publishing*

Web: www.bookleafpub.com

E-mail: info@bookleafpub.com

ISBN: 9789360947606

First edition 2024

*For my mumma & papa, who listened to each
rhyme and all the cut verses.*

ACKNOWLEDGEMENT

Thank you to my mom for pushing me, nudging me and inspiring me to tread upon this path.
Thank you to my dad for listening to my poems even at nightfall after an exhausting flight or a day at the office.
Thank you to my brother for, well, being in my life.
Thank you to all my close friends for listening to me rant about my poetry book and making them listen to these pieces.
And thank you to the flowers and the clouds and the sky and the sea for giving me so much to pen down about.

The Trespasser.

The rusted picture frames sit atop my walls,
mimicking the feeling that within my heart
crawls.

It's said, one romanticises the past &
so I sit bundled up under a bittersweet spell cast.

I glance and then glance again
at my identity card,
Wondering, when did we all
put up this facade?

'Best friends' and 'forever' were words eternally
intertwined,
Just like the arms back then of You & I.

When did classroom giggles turn into just texts
of that kind?
When did we bid adieu to our daily hugs of
goodbye?

And there's a sliver of you
in every nook of my room,
from the screen-recordings,
of our meetings on zoom.

In walled polaroids and
corner folds that adorn my card games.
Kept on the shelves,
you're in my novel's titles and names.

So I sit and open my tattered memory box,
And into my mind,
nostalgia,
trespasses and walks.

Dusk

Orange haze,
Perfect days.

Summer sunsets,
The sky set ablaze.

Captured on phones,
These interlaced
tones.

Yet the tapestry so
stitched,
Could only our eyes,
enrich.

A yearning.

Boredom was analogous to hunger,
a sensation I was supposed to brush off.
Yet somehow, somewhere along the way,
I had moulded that into my bread and water.

Somewhere along the way, boredom had become
what I craved every morning and night.
For it was then when I felt most at peace,
and yet it was now that I was bored the least.

I begged and begged at the feet of divinity to
give me,

just a moment of this peace,
just a sip of this elixir.
Yet something was continuously wheeling
around my mind.
The same way the cars outside my window did.
They honked
and
crashed
and
drove haywire.

loml. (love of my life)

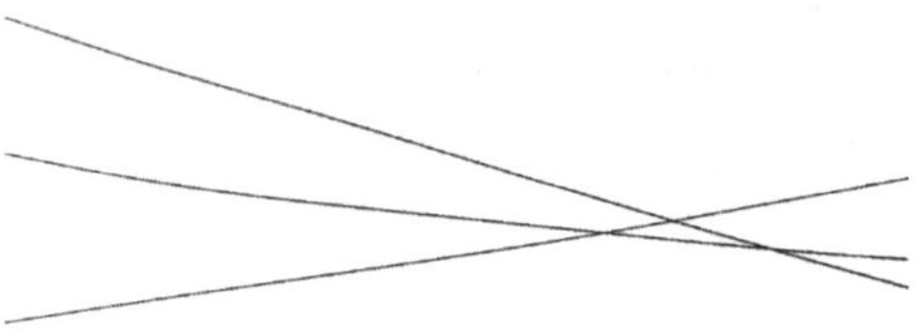

That iconic sea-link and
those irregular shaped "pathars"
Blinking, blurry, yellow-red traffic strings,
woven and stitched.
Those occasional potholes and
open gutters.
A sense of reality and dream together,
forevermore glitched.

A movie scene, me the main character,
the wind and sky and sea and stones, comrades.
The magnetic field of this city—strong.
Attracting, encapsulating, hijacking my being
like a genie in a lamp, as it slowly fades.

Fades and mingles, submerging into that
of this phenomenon.
This phenomenon, this feeling,
this emotion that is Bombay.
Moulding me into herself as one does
their first love, she's mine.
My first love, Bombay.

Pirouettes of the Earth

It's a saying that's said,
'The earth's spinning and so should you.'
But how much ever I may sway and spin
and with whatsoever foot I may tread.
My favourite dance is that of our planet blue.

How each leaf dwindles
and every idyllic droplet sprinkles.

How the ever so glorious fire,
kindles and towers and sets ablaze.
Dying inevitably in the
trickling water's embrace.

The breeze invites my locks
to the dance floor.
They intertwine in a slow waltz,
it's such instances when it strikes me
There's so much more!

So much more to
survive, thrive, and take a chance upon.
So much more to
wake up to, each breaking dawn.

By the film.

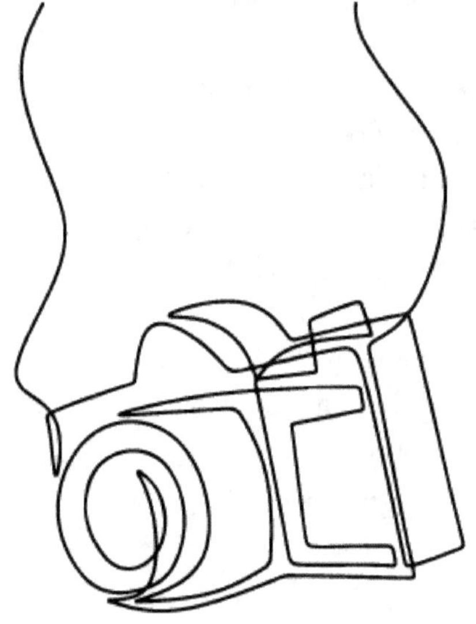

Through some old albums
we flipped.
The joyous moments,
into we dipped.

Chitter and chatter
filled the room,
euphoria settled in
instead of gloom.

Memories, wheeled
into our mind
In life, how much
we find!

Travelled in time,
lots of decades we did.
Mulling, why to these good times,
farewell we bid?

Scottishite.

Across the room,
Paper balls flew.
For extra 5 minutes of break,
The teacher we'd try to woo.

The agony inflicting, sultry assemblies,
We hated.
To contest with our chatter,
"PIN DROP SILENCE" the teachers stated.

"Is this a fish market?"
"Do you forget to eat?"
Were phrases that
We'd all routinely greet.

It was the gossip
At lunches.

Mingled with daily episodes,
Of thrown punches.

Often were taken trips,
To the nurse's office.
In the bins, entombed were
our pen-fight warriors corpses.

The tie and sash and tunic.
We'd wear.
I miss the days of the,
Scholastic book fair.

Tiffin boxes, notebooks and
exam pads became bats.

And the ever so important,
'Odd-Eve' stats.

Frankies with friends outside school,
were the tradition and custom.
To saying goodbye to this place,
How will I ever get accustomed?

Balance?

Yellow and white boxes,
Adorn the concrete towers.
As blue onsets in the sky,
The red lights up on cars.

Even as the clock strikes eleven at night,
There's a busy hustle in the air.
Even as kids sleep,
The workers work till their hands go bare.

In this city of dreams,
Some walk home with
Meagre rupees in their pockets.
While some go to lavish parties,
With champagne and gold lockets.

This is the reality of,
The city I live in.
But after all this is balance,
the intertwined yang and yin.

Power is Fleeting.

In earth, water, wind, fire
there's power,
But each flame burns to the ground
no matter how tall it shall tower.

Each storm ceases,
Each mountain degrades.
Each flood decreases,
Each tree leaf fades.

Pride comes before a fall they say,
but can you put power and greed at bay.
For if you don't, nature will,
And her goal she shall always fulfil.

Now or Never.

By a Big Bang, it was created,
But, we thrive or help her survive has been
lately debated.
Million years ago, our Earth came into
existence,
But now in saving her we shall not show
resistance.

Years have passed, and there are years to come,
It's now in our hands what our planet shall
become.
A barren land filled with drought and famine?
Why do we divide things into YOURS and
MINE?

Instead, let's join our hands,
It's time to save our Mother Earth.
So everyone, plant a tree on the lands,
Let's save the mother who, to us gave birth!

Who Would've Thought?

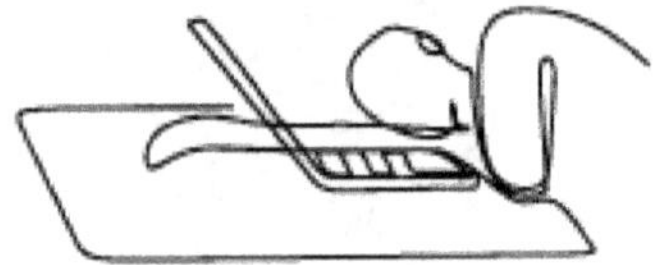

Who would have thought we would
Do school in our own houses.
Without the fun, the sharing of lunch,
Just with keyboards and mouses.

No passing notes, no whispering,
No blackboard monitors as well.
Just sitting on a chair and table,
Instead of running when we would hear the
recess bell.

At first it was a dream come true
And we just wanted it forever,
But now I say what before
I thought in my life I would never

I want to go to offline school
No matter if only for a year!
I miss the stick on the wall and chip-chop craze.
These memories I hold dear.

Afghanistan, 2021.

After 20 years we are back to square one
What is this, what is this, what is this we've
done?

Blaming it on others is a cowardly crutch
It's not solely about countries and politics but
our society's thinking is such.

Our interpretation and somewhat misogynist
deeds
That is what on which, all wrongdoers feed.

A country instead of taking one step forward is
stepping 200 years back!
We have to 'together' get this world back on
track.

If only Pangea hadn't broken up
Would we then walk together with our hands
held and heads up

Of all genders and religions and tribes and races
Would we yet hate individuals just by the
colours of their faces?

Change is now and we do have the potential,
But taking the first step ourselves is essential.

Teachers.

From abc to H_2O
Thank you teachers,
for helping us grow.

Our doubts you cleared and
Problems helped solve
Taught us good manners and
Guided us to evolve

At times we surely made a few mistakes,
And sat in the staff room during our breaks.

In the end, you always forgave us and made us
smile
Taught us with utmost enthusiasm no matter
how big was your correction pile

You taught us things we shall always remember.
Along with book learning, the dance steps for
the annual concert in December
And although online learning was hard for us
both
You never let that obstruct our learning and
growth.

An Eternal Duet

In the sky's ballet, they dance.
A boon,
The sun's halcyon blaze,
the moon's ivory swoon.

They share the sky, each with its own light.
A timeless canvas, painted in celestial delight.

Their silent symphony orchestrates the show.
In harmony they exist and balance they bestow.

As dawn births dusk and dusk to dawn,
Their undying rhythm carries forever on.

Sukoon.

It's the tranquil sunset in a traffic jam.
It's the extra 5 minutes of sleep.
It's that one star shining brighter in the sky.
It's the old songs in my playlist I keep.

It cradles me in a sense of peace and comfort.
It's a funny feeling that wheels around my mind.
It's a respite from monotony.
It's the grey clouds that are silverlined.

It's the 'sukoon' in the chaos.

My gaze.

At times I compel myself to
Look through a poet's lens,
To see the world in a certain
Romantic sense.

To record on these pages,
The poppies at my door.
Sketch with words how the fire rages,
And the romping waves ashore.

The lanes of Bombay,
And the classic taxis that roam.
The cracks running down old architecture
Imprison in my verses that feeling of 'home'

And that's when it strikes me
I needn't force myself to paint my view as such
For my stripped iris alone
Holds the same poetic touch.

infinity

infinity.
A word. One with countable letters
Yet encompassing in its meaning, the
uncountable.
infinity.
Found in every point and every number and
Every thought of which one is capable.
infinity.
Of different sizes and yet both countless
infinity.
Harnessing the power of the boundless.

Christmas in Mumbai?

Snowflakes sure seem to be amiss
But still the feeling settles right in
The laughter echoing engulfing the room
Familiarises a sense of bliss

A cosy hug, the woollen stockings,
Is it me or does even the air seem warmer?
Outside chilly but in its heart a snugly charm,
the fairy lights grace the ceilings along

The moon drags by and the city tumbles into one
lit as though by fireflies.
A Diwali after-party?
These moments sit so precious and lit pleasantly
dim,

I wish each one I could carve, inscribe and print
down on film.

Christmas in Mumbai is like no other
The marine drive air still wafts up my nose,
The heat still enough to switch on the AC at
night,
Yet there's this aura of festivity that everybody
knows.

It's the ooze of the dishes at every Christmas
breakfast, dinner and lunch.
It's the long anticipated family brunch.
It's the crunch of the dead leaves the little kids
giggle and scamper over.
It's the season of *adrak wali chai* coupled with a
gingerbread house, sweet and sober.

From the decorations to the Starbucks cups all
sit in the
Attire of red, green and white.
This season wherever in the world just
Gift wraps the world in zeal and light.

Dil-wali Diwali.

The cotton candy clouds ambushed the flight,
as we in awe looked at the view.
Nose scrunched up, mouth-chewing gum,
we reached our destination
to the sky bidding adieu.

Minutes elapsed in a blink of an eye,
as the car came to a screeching halt.
After a long day on the road and up high,
we finally reached Home! Home it was called …

As the great orange ball of fire dipped into
profound sleep,
The city lit up with diyas to vanish the darkness
deep.
A bindi, a lehenga, eyeliner (kohl) on my eyelid,
There was celebration, laughter and giggles
amid.

It's Time.

Running like a river,
Finally, I'm free.
You may capture me for a while,
But you can't contain me.

Flying like the air.
Flowing like the water.
But firm like the Earth bare.
Still, can't be oppressed like fire's daughter.

Like an uncaged bird,
I'll glide towards the Sun.
Or with the moon, I'll dance up high,
To put me down there are none.

Freedom is when there's a free will.
When opinions aren't a crime.
Your mind is seized until...
You decide it's time!

It's time to show your feelings,
It's time to show your emotion,
It's time that people can be who they are
without any commotion!
It's time.

Who Am I?

It's in the afternoons when,
Greener is the grass's hue.
The wind twirls like a ballerina then,
And the sun pierces the velvet blue.

Waves roll in the distant sea,
Who am I? And who must I be?

I am all the people I've met,
And the experiences shared.
The shooting stars I watch jet,

and all the stuff toys for whom I've cared.

The sunsets and moon phases,
And the skies I star gaze.
Old diaries I read through,
In a bittersweet daze.

All the friends I've made,
And the pieces of persona we've bartered.
Snippets of myself, along with them fade,
Yet remain etched in my being are the moments
we chartered.

My favourite colour now yellow,
For it reminds me of a friend.
I'd hated lychee flavoured jell-o,
but she made me love it in the end.

I am all the smiles I've seen,
And the tears I've wiped.
The shoulders on which my head's been,
And all the poems I've typed.